TEACHER'S GUIDE
TO
AUTISTIC BEHAVIOR:
What, why and how to help

by
Dr. Heather MacKenzie

Wired Fox Publications

Library and Archives of Canada Cataloguing in Publi-cation

TEACHER'S GUIDE TO AUTISTIC BEHAVIOR: What, why and how to help

Heather MacKenzie

ISBN 978-0-9684466-9-0

Dedication

This book is dedicated to Christin Scholten (1978-2018). Christin prompted me to put my thoughts and experiences together with her many questions about the young adults she loved teaching. I was honored to be "Your Other Mother" and thank you for prompting me to put my little bits of wisdom into print.

Love you forever, Christin!

Acknowledgements

There are many people I need to thank. They all play roles in sustaining my energy in this field of autism and in inducing me to refine my approaches.

First, I need to thank my long-suffering husband, Bill. He often experiences blank stares from me in the middle of conversations when my brain wanders to issues I'm puzzling through.

My dear friend Susan Deike is the best editor ever. She's eagle-eyed and helps my writing flow. She is the protectrice of the Oxford comma and a guardian of the Gricean principle of avoiding prolixity.

There are many more people who've helped me bring this guide to fruition:

Marian Baronit, your input about teaching and teacher viewpoints was invaluable.

To my wonderful friend and colleague, Chris Barson, you are a guiding light. Your passion for autism is palpable and your willingness to share your knowledge is deeply appreciated.

Gordon Bullivant, your vision, wisdom, and undying enthusiasm give me a boost and greater perseverance in our shared mission to make learning better for all students.

Debby Elley, I thank you for your input and support. Your knowledge of the lived experience brings such wisdom and good humor.

Dr. Teeya Scholten, my sage colleague and friend, you help me keep up my motivation and my conceptual clarity.

Margie Rice, you are a teacher's teacher. Thank you for your insights and support.

Michele Barlow and Martha Giles, thank you for prompting me to complete this guide. And many thanks to Sue Grierson for bringing me together with Michele and Martha.

Contents

Introduction

This guide takes a serious look at behavior in students with autism and related conditions[1].

My goal is to help teachers[2] look at behavior differently. I don't want children to just become compliant. My focus is on helping them learn to become masters of their own behavior, thinking, and emotions. This means helping you understand what behavior is, how to look at it, and how to help children help themselves.

The first thing we'll look at is whether a behavior truly is a problem. This is an important issue because not all things classified as behaviors are problems. Some are a little odd. Some are mildly irritating. But they're not really problem behaviors.

Then we'll look at executive functions and self-regulation. I describe executive functions and the vital role they play in many of the behaviors we see in students with autism. These include difficulties with planning and organization as well as impulse control. Memory and self-monitoring also play important roles. Rigid thinking is another issue that impacts students' ability to regulate their behavior, thinking, and emotions.

Following that, we'll look at the relationship between behavior and stress. Anxiety is common in students with autism. It reduces their ability to self-regulate. Because of this, it increases the likelihood of problem behaviors. Their ability to cope and to learn becomes seriously eroded. Common stressors for students with autism are outlined, as are distress reactions.

Next, we take a look at the boredom-to-distress continuum. One of our goals is to help students expand their feelings of optimal wellbeing ('just right'). Mindful breathing is presented as an effective way to do this. In this section, we discuss how to introduce and practice mindful breathing with students. Once they experience a sense of calm, we'll focus on helping them identify signs of boredom and distress in their bodies.

This enables them to alert themselves and using appropriate strategies. Four main strategies for regaining self-regulation and a sense of just right' are presented in the chapter.

The next section presents four ways to help students deal with behaviors you've identified as problems. They include simple behavior rules, expanded behavior rules, Social Stories™, and problem solving.

Following this are ways to help students once they've had a behavioral event, a meltdown. We know that we can't prevent all difficulties. We can, however, do specific things to help them dissipate.

The final chapter reviews some of the key points addressed in this guide.

---

[1] Throughout, I'll use the term 'autism' but all strategies can be used with children who have related conditions. They're also sound strategies for any students but my main focus will be on those with exceptional needs.

[2] My main audience is teachers but this guide will help anyone who wants to help children with autism in positive, productive ways become masters of their own behavior, thinking and emotions.

Behavior – problem or not?

Behavior is any action or reaction to something. It can be a reaction to something going on inside the person. It can be something going on outside.

In students with autism, a lot goes on inside that you might not even notice. Sometimes, this internalized behavior can go on for a long time before you're aware of it. It just builds and builds. You might notice small changes in the student. They may chew their sleeves or pencils, or they might stick more rigidly to routines and ways of doing things. This slow build-up can make it difficult to figure out what caused a behavior. It's not always a simple issue of figuring out what happened just before – that may simply be the thing that triggered the behavior.

Externalized behavior is usually either self-directed or directed at other people or things.

Self-directed behavior can include hand flapping, humming, shrieking or pacing. Some self-directed behaviors can be harmful, such as when students bite themselves or bang their heads.

Externalized behavior directed at people or things might include yelling at or hitting another person. It may include throwing things, tossing a chair or tearing a book.

I've learned that behavior in students with autism shouldn't be classified as 'good' or 'bad' or even necessarily a 'problem'. Behavior is communication. The student is trying to tell you how they feel about things going on around them. They may not be able to explain it in words but their behavior shows it.

When is behavior a problem?

A problem behavior is one that:

1. interferes with the student's learning and/or ability to do an activity of daily living (such as functional or leisure activities),

2. interferes with other students' learning and/or other people's ability to do an activity of daily living,

3. causes a situation that could be dangerous or unsafe, and/or

4. is socially and/or culturally inappropriate or unacceptable.

This definition refocuses the meaning of problem behavior. It says that 'unconventional' behavior is okay. A behavior may seem a bit 'odd' but, if it doesn't interfere with learning or other activities, isn't dangerous, and isn't socially unacceptable, it's not a problem.

Look at the behaviors in the table below and see what you think.

Behavior	Interferes with learning or activity		Dangerous or unsafe	Socially/ culturally not appropriate/ acceptable	Problem?
	Student	Other students			
Student wants to stand rather than sit in the classroom	✗	✗	✗	✗	no
Student wants to work under a desk or a table	✗	✗	✗	?	Probably not
Student is talking loudly to themselves and can't seem to get started with an activity	✓	?	✗	?	yes
Student throws a piece of equipment	✓	✓	✓	?	Yes
Student self-stimulates by twirling string in front of their face	✓	✗	✗	?	Maybe

Weigh each factor separately and consider the importance to that student, their peer group and their family. For example, if a behavior is dangerous, then it's a problem regardless of the other factors. If the behavior is socially- or culturally-inappropriate for a family, then it's a problem, regardless of the other factors.

Here's the first example: a student prefers to stand rather than sit while doing a task. Is that a problem? I don't think so. I've met teachers who got into battles of will with students just because the students preferred to stand. If it's not interfering with anyone's learning, why even pay attention to it? In fact, some people find they're more alert and able to learn when standing.

What if a student wants to sit under a desk or table? That's probably not a problem either.

If a student is talking loudly to themselves and can't seem to move on, that's a problem. They're likely distracting other students, as well as getting stuck.

A student who throws a piece of equipment is interfering with everyone's learning. Also, flying equipment is potentially dangerous. That behavior is a problem.

If a student self-stimulates ('stims') by rocking, flapping, twirling a piece of string, it likely interferes with their learning. It may or may not interfere with other students and it's not dangerous. It may, however, marginalize them socially and make other students fearful of them. This isn't a black-and-white situation. Stims are pleasurable releases for people with autism. This means that addressing them as 'problem behaviors' needs careful consideration and discussion with parents before proceeding (see Chapter 6 for a simple strategy that may help).

Deciding if something is socially- or culturally-appropriate is a difficult issue. Check with each family to see what's acceptable within their culture. Always be careful not to impose your own beliefs and customs on other people. Each culture is different. When it comes to the culture of your school, that's where you can decide. Use your knowledge of your school to decide what's acceptable and what's not, what might marginalize the person and what won't.

Keep in mind that problem behaviors aren't a matter of your personal preferences, desires, or perceptions. You may find something a little 'odd' or even irritating. Keep your cool and go through the checklist in the table on page 4. Make your decision objectively: does the behavior interfere with learning? is it dangerous? is it inappropriate?

One of my favorite quotes about behavior that made an impact on my own practices comes from Dr. Carl Haywood, of Vanderbilt University. He warned:

> *"... recognize that the student's behavior is neither random nor malicious but is motivated by some need, wish or impulse that .... might be worth considering."*

I've heard teachers, parents, and caregivers say that a student is being 'manipulative' or 'stubborn' or is 'trying to make my life difficult'. I remember one teacher who told me there was nothing wrong with the seven-year-old child I was observing in her classroom. She said, "He just lacks a work ethic." He actually had a severe learning disability. She saw the child's behavior as a disruption in her class. Her words really came from her frustration in not meeting the child's need. Her failure to see the real causes made my heart ache.

So-called problem behavior is really the student's attempt to communicate some need or feeling. Our role is to look and to try to figure out what they're communicating. We need to recognize that there's something legitimate going on. Carl Haywood said it best:

> *"... behavior is seldom just plain bad but is more often ill-timed or set in the wrong place or directed inappropriately."*

The Role of Executive Functions

What are executive functions?

Executive functions are brain processes that make it possible to turn ideas and goals into actions. They're mainly located in your frontal lobes (just behind your forehead – the darker area in the picture to the right).

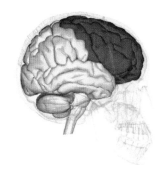

Executive functions help you put things you know into actions. They take you from knowing or intending to do something to doing it. They complete the connection between your knowledge and your actions.

There are five key executive functions that make this connection happen. They include:

1. **Planning and organization.** This involves managing and putting thoughts and intentions into step-by-step plans.

2. **Inhibitory control** lets you push away thoughts, emotions, and actions that might interfere with what you're doing. It also stops behavior that's not helpful and lets you keep going with things even if they're difficult.

3. **Working memory** is a temporary storage system. It lets you take in information and hold it in your mind. Then you can update and put things together.

4. **Self-monitoring** is the ability to supervise actions and thoughts, and notice when there's a problem. It lets you keep an eye on the quality and accuracy of what you're doing.

5. **Cognitive flexibility** is the ability to move from one rule, situation, or activity to another when things change. It lets you adapt to the unfamiliar or unexpected. It also prompts you to change old ideas or ways of doing things and put them together to make new ones.

Have a look at the maze below. If I want to complete it, what do I need to do? I have to get myself organized - what do I need? - a pencil and, thinking ahead, an eraser would be a good idea. I need to control my impulses that make me want to add a sun to the sky and bigger flowers.

I plan to start by drawing with my finger first, moving to the right to see where it leads me. I have to stick to the plan and goal in my working memory as I move along. Oops, I keep running into dead ends. Self-monitoring made me realize I need to stop and change my plan. I need to keep my thinking flexible enough to stop what I'm doing and try a new approach.

What's the connection between executive functions and self-regulation?

Self-regulation is the ability to consciously control your executive functions. Self-regulation lets you control and tune your behavior, thinking, and emotions to different situations in healthy and appropriate ways. Self-regulation is taking control of your executive functions and making them work for you - not just leaving things to chance.

By developing self-regulation skills:

- Your behavior, thoughts, and emotions don't rule you.

- You become more self-directed, planful, adaptable. You don't need someone constantly telling you what to do and not do.

- You understand the relationship between effort and achievement. You learn what it takes to do what you want.

Remember, self-regulation isn't just self-control. Children need to use all five executive functions.

Children also need to know when NOT to use self-regulation. They need to learn when they can let loose, be loud, and active.

Self-Regulation takes time to develop

Executive functions and self-regulation typically develop and mature over a long period of time.

Developing and refining self-regulation takes at least the first two decades of life. Each of the five key executive functions develops at a different pace; some mature earlier, some later.

The diagram below shows that self-regulation starts developing at birth and doesn't mature until at least the mid-twenties. Development reflects changes in the maturation of the brain's frontal lobes.

Infants may suck their fingers and thumbs to regulate and soothe themselves. That's beginning self-regulation.

Preschoolers show a surge in their abilities to control their bodies. Regulating their emotions also begins to mature. Attention becomes more focused and children can concentrate for longer periods of time.

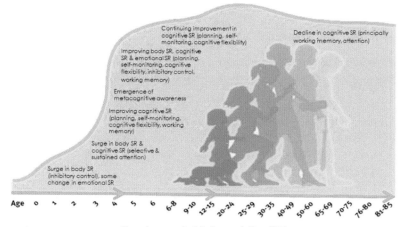

Development of Self-regulation (SR)

In later preschool years, cognitive self-regulation shows greater improvements. Children are better at planning and organizing themselves and things they want to do. Their working memory improves and they're self-monitoring more. Their improved cognitive flexibility means they can change plans and approaches more easily. One really important change in the later preschool years is the emergence of

9

metacognitive awareness. That is, children become aware of their thinking; what helps them remember, what makes it harder to learn.

Self-regulation of behavior, thinking, and emotions continues to improve during the school years. There's a small dip during the teen years - ask any parent of a teenager what that's about - but it's followed by continuing refinement.

Remember, self-regulation takes at least the first two decades of life to mature. This reflects brain development. We shouldn't expect self-regulation to appear overnight. New nerve pathways are developing and strengthening as children learn and practice skills.

Keep in mind that some children will need to 'un-learn' old ways of doing things before they can develop new approaches. This will take more time and effort before you can move on to improving self-regulation.

The autism-self-regulation connection

The more I've worked with people with autism, the more I realize that problems with self-regulation play a central role. Children with autism have varying difficulties in most of the five key executive functions and it shows in their behavior.

By definition, children with autism:

- **Have difficulty with back-and-forth interactions with other people.** Difficulties with 'social back-and-forth' is likely related to problems regulating their attention. When attention is scattered, it's hard to figure out important cues. Problems with interacting are also related to inconsistent self-monitoring ("what's going on here?", "what do I need to do?") as well as poor working memory ("what was that?") and cognitive flexibility ("I need to change what I'm doing.").

- **Become over-focused on specific thoughts and ideas.** This laser focus seems to be a combination of difficulty with inhibitory control ("I can't stop myself from doing what I'm doing"), self-monitoring ("I'm not aware that I keep thinking about the same things"), and cognitive flexibility ("I'm stuck!").

- **Prefer to stick to the same way of doing things.** If planning and organizing are problems, isn't it easier to stick to the same old ways of doing things? When you can't focus (inhibit) your attention and you're pulled in too many directions, doesn't it feel better to stick with ways you know? These are all self-regulation issues.

- **Do the same actions or use the same words and phrases over and over.** Repetitive behaviors, like hand flapping or talking about the same topic, are likely related to problems with inhibitory control ("I can't stop myself") and self-monitoring ("what do you mean I do this all the time?"). It also points to problems with cognitive flexibility ("I can't shift to other thoughts or actions").

Other behaviors, such as unusual eating habits, disrupted sleep patterns, self-harm, and extreme temper tantrums are probably related to difficulties with self-regulation.

Difficulty with self-regulation might not explain all characteristics and behaviors of children with autism but it is compelling. Experience has shown that work on executive functions has far-reaching impact on all of these features. If you work with children to improve their inhibitory control, you'll see benefits in other executive functions. If you work on one executive function, you'll see pay-offs in other areas.

The Relationship between Behavior & Stress

Behaviors often arise as students become anxious and stressed. We know that up to 80% of people with autism experience high levels of anxiety. When you're anxious, your self-regulation goes out the window. You're more likely to behave impulsively or more rigidly.

Not all stress is bad, though. The word 'stress' is seen as negative by most people. But stress really is anything that thrills us, worries us, scares us or threatens us. Stress can be a strong motivator and energizer ..... at the right intensity.

Anxiety, however, comes from too much stress or stress over a long time. Here, we use the terms 'anxiety' and 'distress' to describe those high levels of stress. They're the ones that can undermine our sense of security and cause disruptions in our lives.

Things that affect stress tolerance

We all need a certain amount of stress to stimulate us and keep us alert.

For students with autism, optimal levels depend on a few key things:

1. **Physical state**

   Student. Are they well-rested? Did they eat within the last two to three hours? Are they feeling well? Are they wearing comfortable (not itchy or sticky) clothing? Are they warm or cool enough? Are they thirsty? Did they have a change in medication or start a new medication?

   I use the acronym C.A.N. (as in the student 'can' learn) to remind myself that students must be **C**alm, **A**lert, and **N**ourished. When students aren't Calm, Alert, and Nourished, they can slip into boredom or distress easily.

Teacher. If you aren't Calm, Alert, and Nourished, you also can slip out of your own optimal 'just right' state. You can have low energy, or you can slip into distress if you haven't looked after your own needs.

2. **Emotional state**

   Student. If students are having difficulties in other areas of their lives, they'll have problems staying in an optimal state. The same goes for things that happened in the past. Something can trigger an old memory that sets the student off. Some days, students with autism just wake up feeling 'grouchy' for no apparent reason.

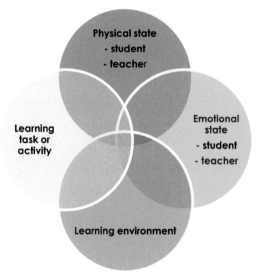

Key factors affecting stress tolerance

   Teacher. Students with autism can be 'emotional sponges'. They absorb emotions around them and won't necessarily understand what or why. Your emotional state is critical to your students' emotional state.

3. **Learning environment.** When the learning environment is calm and feels secure to the students, their optimal energy range can grow. If it feels chaotic and disorganized, students can become distressed more easily.

4. **Learning task/activity.** If a task is new to the student, it can stress some and distress others. Is it new to the student and

potentially stressful? Is it something they've done many times in the past and is boring? Is it challenging but not too challenging? Do they have to use verbal or fine motor skills that are areas of difficulty for them? Is it taking too long to finish the task? Does the student fully understand what's expected? Is it something they hate doing? If the student has enjoyed and been successful with this sort of task in the past, they're more likely to be alert and ready to learn. If it's in an area of high interest for that student, you'll see a wonderful flow of energy level.

Extra stressors for students with autism

Stressors can push students into a state of distress and anxiety. That means they're pushed out of the zone where they can learn most effectively and efficiently. When they hit distress, they're over-stimulated and/or overwhelmed. Learning isn't going to happen.

For people with autism, stressors are things that violate their need for clarity, precision, planfulness, and logical decision-making. In the table below are some of the typical stressors for students with autism.

Typical Stressors for students with autism	Examples
Things are poorly organized	Materials, tasks and activities aren't clearly organized or defined Schedules or plans aren't followed Personal belongings aren't consistently in the same location
Tasks are vague with poorly-defined standards, expectations, goals, priorities	There are too many options for activities; procedures and goals are left open-ended; materials are presented in no particular order There is no clear order to tasks or daily life; no agenda, schedule or plan
Decisions and methods are based on opinion or guesses rather than reasoning and logic	"I just want you to do it this way"; "Let's try it this way this time.", "Do this" (without explanation)
Other people's incomplete or imprecise work impacts the quality of their work	Piece of equipment is missing; a word is misspelled or missing Others don't do a task exactly as the student expects or has in mind

Typical Stressors for students with autism	Examples
Student is asked to 'wing it' - the reality and facts of the situation are ignored	"Don't worry, it'll be okay this way.", "That's good enough.", "It doesn't need to be perfect."; "Just ignore that."
Sudden change without forewarning and/or good rationale	"I changed my mind", "We aren't going to do that today after all.". A substitute teacher or other staff just shows up with no forewarning. Student hasn't completed a task to their satisfaction but is told to move on
New possibilities are presented to the student after they've already made up their mind	"How about we do it this way?"; "Let's do it tomorrow", "Let's do this instead."
Too many details or too much information is presented to them	"Then we can do this and this and this....."; "Get your __, then ___, then ___, then ___"
Working too long or too hard without a break	Student has used a lot of energy on an activity and is expected to do more.
High level of competition	Pressing the student to complete a task faster, more accurately, or within a very short time limit.

Individual students will vary in terms of their personal triggers. To understand each student, complete the Survey of Stressors (in Appendix I). The survey lists a variety of social, environmental, health, and sensory issues commonly identified as stressors by people with autism. It will help you identify key stressors. Be sure to get input from the students and their parents.

Some Signs of Distress in Students with Autism

Once a student with autism goes beyond an optimal level of stimulation, it's usually not a long way to a 'distress' reaction.

First signs of distress and anxiety in students with autism are often sensory. They may chew pencils, spin objects, pace, flap their hands, or become over-focused on small details. Raw emotions may take over, with the student melting down, becoming increasingly rigid, and/or extremely fearful. They may panic and feel like their entire world is falling apart.

The table below presents some common distress reactions. Always keep in mind that each student's distress reaction will vary. Those presented in the table are ones I've seen most frequently. Watch each student to figure out how they typically react to the stressors.

Typical Distress Reactions in people with autism	Examples
Focus on sensations through touch, taste, smell, movement, hearing or vision	Chew clothing, fingers or fingernails, flap hands, suck objects, pace, bang head, hit or flick objects repeatedly
Focus on details and facts	Organize and re-organize possessions and tools; over-focus on details; criticize lack of detail, such as on a schedule
Distrust their understanding of details and have difficulty focusing on relevant information	Become upset over seemingly trivial things, such as the wrong kind of pencil; worry about their ability to finish a task
Become impulsive and act without thinking	Hit, kick, or bite themselves or someone else; make hurtful comments to others
Experience confusion, anxiety and panic even if appearing outwardly calm	Start chewing things; their body may tighten up; pupils may dilate
Become negative, unwilling to tolerate anything unknown or unfamiliar, sometimes unwilling to accept even known, familiar and enjoyable activities	Student doesn't want to get a favorite treat; refuses or becomes upset at the mention of favorite or familiar things
Erupt into extreme, harsh reactions	Student has a melt down; critical of people and activities around them
Imagine disastrous outcomes and see previously safe places and/or people as being dangerous or frightening	Student fears other students or teachers; worries there are dangerous people, animals or objects that might hurt them
Resist even minor changes in routines, procedures, and goals	Rejects even fairly small suggestions like "How about if we do this first?"
Begin to lose things, blame others for the loss	"I can't find my shoes. They're gone. Somebody took them!"
Over-focus on things causing stress, unable to relax	"It'll never get better"; "They'll take my things again tomorrow"
Become silent and unwilling to talk about stresses	"Nothing's wrong"; "Let me alone"; may hide
Try to avoid a stressful situation or task	"I don't want to go to the studio"; may run away and hide
Blame other people or objects for the difficulty; become suspicious about other people's intentions	"They keep taking my things"; "My teacher said I can't do that."

Learning to self-regulate mood

If we can help students with autism to keep from slipping into distress and anxiety, we've come a long way to improving their learning and general well-being.

One of the most interesting things I've learned from people with autism is that they typically have difficulty identifying their own rising stress. Also, they can go through a distress reaction and have no idea what happened. They didn't see it coming and didn't realize when it happened. It's not a cover-up. They really don't recognize these things.

How can you work on something that flies through their systems like a secret storm?

Boredom, stress, distress

In everyone's life, there's a continuum from no stress and boredom to too much stress, distress, and anxiety. The diagram to the right shows the continuum.

In most people, low arousal/alertness leads to boredom and poor attention. As arousal/stress increases so does performance ... to a point. Once a certain level of stress/arousal is reached, performance and learning drop off.

With autistic people, the slip from optimal 'just right' performance into distress and anxiety is often a quick and slippery slope. That means the middle 'just right' window is often quite narrow.

We need to help students with autism in three main ways:

1.   **Increase their ability to self-calm.** By teaching a calming strategy, we help students improve their ability to cope with stress. They build a sense of calm that helps them cope.

2.   **Learn to identify their mood.** Autistic students usually have a lot of trouble identifying how they're feeling. They may not know when they're slipping into boredom or distress. They often don't have a clear idea of how it feels to be 'just right'.

3.   **Improve their ability to self-regulate their mood.** It's critical that we teach students strategies for regulating their mood so they can return to an optimal 'just right' state. We need to extend the middle section of the diagram above as well as help them deal with stress and boredom.

All the strategies described in this chapter take time and repeated practice before students can use them on their own. Always keep in mind that there will likely be backslides when the student is affected by any of the issues described on pages 13 through 15.

1.   Increase the student's ability to self-calm

The best ways to help students avoid and deal with stress and anxiety are proactive and focused on preventing problems.

One of the most effective techniques to help anyone become more resilient to stress is mindfulness. Mindfulness[3] helps us focus on the 'here and now' and let other things flow away. It helps calm both our mind and body.

Mindfulness has some excellent features for people with autism. First of all, mindfulness is a simple sensory-based process – you use simple sensations to guide your attention. It's nonverbal and doesn't require anything but paying attention to what you do anyway – breathe.

By teaching mindfulness, your students will learn what 'calm' feels like. I've found that most people with autism can't identify where stress and anxiety are in their bodies. Ask them where they feel stress and either they'll say they don't know or they'll point to various body parts. They probably spend so much of their lives in states of anxiety it's hard to tell what 'un-stressed' feels like.

A simple introduction to mindfulness

Here's a simple introduction to teaching mindfulness to your students.

Find a quiet place where you won't be disturbed. The space should be as uncluttered as possible – a place where distractions are minimized.

Start in a comfortable sitting position. Sit on the floor with a pillow or in a comfortable chair. The most important things are that your student is able to sit up straight, be comfortable and feel that their body is secure and well-grounded.

Make sure they're neither too warm nor too cool.

Turn down the lights. Students can shut their eyes if that makes concentrating easier.

Play soft music if that helps. Have a look at the free app *Relax Melodies*[4] that lets you mix and listen to many different relaxing sounds.

Make up your own script for guiding your students. A typical script goes something like this: softly and in simple terms talk to your students about paying attention to the air coming in through their nose: "Let the air come in slowly through your nose … (inhale)1, 2, 3. Now, hold your breath … 1, 2, 3 then exhale slowly. Feel the air coming out of your nose." Focus on the sensation of breathing.

There are apps that can help guide you and your students in their mindful breathing. I've suggested a few on the next two pages[5]. Test each one out and see which one(s) work best for individual students.

Some apps that can help with mindful breathing

I tried out each one and gave my evaluation. Try them out for yourself.

Breathing Zone

Description: guides you through simple breathing exercises. You determine the speed of breathing and the length of each session. There is a visual cue that enlarges and diminishes with each intake or expiration of breath. There's also a calm voice that simply says, "Breathe in, breathe out." – it can be turned off if you prefer.
Age range: 4 years and up
Format: iOS and Android
Cost: free
Evaluation: Very simple. The ability to change breathing rate and length of session gives lots of flexibility. The simple language and visual cue are helpful and not distracting.

Calm

Description: guided meditation for beginners, as well as intermediate and advanced users. Sessions are available in lengths of 3, 5, 10, 15, 20 or 25 minutes.
Age range: 4 years and up
Format: iOS and Android
Cost: free (some features)
Evaluation: instructions are a little chatty and not well suited to young children and/or children who have language processing difficulties. With proper adult guidance, it could be useful.

DreamyKid

Description: offers meditation, guided visualization and affirmations for children and teens.
Age range: 2 years to 18
Format: iOS
Cost: free (some features)
Evaluation: nice feature allows you to add and then control the volume of background sounds; peaceful (not gimmicky) meditations that would be more suitable for children from 8 years and up.

Headspace: Guided Meditation and Mindfulness

Description: offers guided meditation
Age range: 4 years of age and up
Format: iOS
Cost: free
Evaluation: a little chatty about all sorts of things other than breathing which may complicate things for kids with autism.

Coach your students to let thoughts and other senses that might enter their minds while they're breathing to float away: "If you get distracted by some ideas that come into your brain, just let them float away like logs on a stream (or clouds in the sky). Watch them float away. Now bring your attention back to your breathing.

Start practicing for two minutes. Then move up to five minutes. Make sure you keep the breathing slow and steady.

Mindful breathing is really simple but it does take practice. Jon Kabat-Zinn, one of the main proponents of mindfulness, points out that mindfulness is different from our natural tendency to exist in our thinking minds. Our minds are typically focused on what should have been done and what needs to be done. In order to keep our minds focused on the here and now you have to practice and put effort into it.

2. Learn to identify mood state

After you've practiced mindful breathing and you see that your students are getting the idea, it's time to identify what it feels like to have a calm brain and body. By learning to detect early signs of oncoming distress or boredom, the students will be better able to prevent it.

Look at the diagrams[6] below. They show where in our bodies most people experience low energy, optimal energy, and distress. You can see how, in a state of distress, many people feel tightness in their chests and stomach as well as their heads.

Ask each student where in their bodies they feel stress. Use the pictures in the diagram to guide them. Explain that some people feel stress in their necks. Some people feel it in their heads. Some people feel it in their stomachs. It's different for everyone but usually centers around your head, chest, and stomach. If students have problems figuring out where they feel stress, do some mindful breathing and then check in again.

Body sensations typically related to different mood states		
Boredom 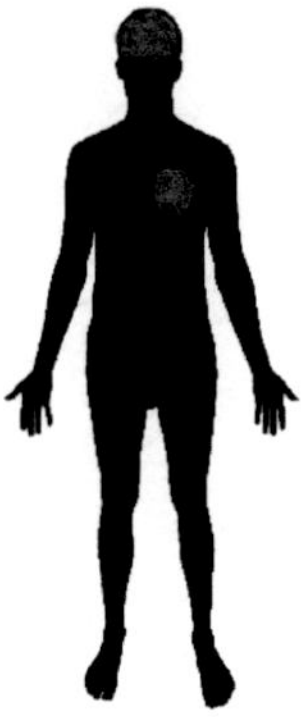	**Optimal 'just right'** 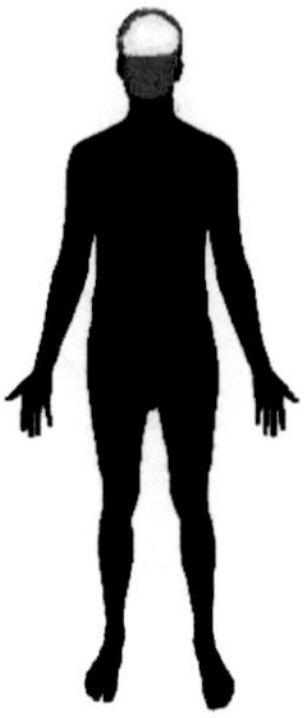	**Distress** 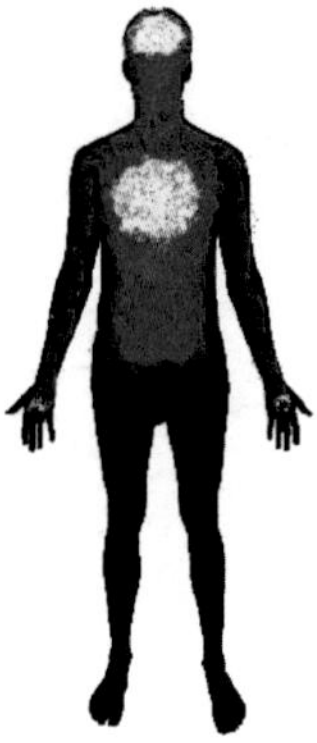

Ask how their bodies feel when they're bored. Contrast that to how their bodies feel when they're calm and ready to learn.

Then see if they can localize stress in their bodies. Tell them they're warning signals for when they need to help themselves regain their calmness.

To make this activity more enduring, have each student complete their own stress meter (example is on the next page, a blank one for you to reproduce is in Appendix II).

The **gray area** on the left side is when they feel bored. Ask each student to tell how their bodies and brains feel when they're bored. Have them write on the stress meter what they feel. You might want to have each student take a selfie of themselves when they feel bored. Add it to the meter.

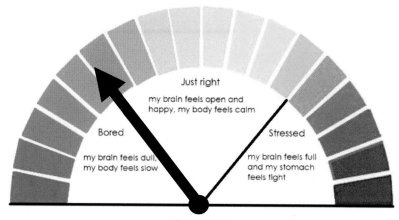

Just right

my brain feels open and
happy, my body feels calm

Bored

my brain feels dull,
my body feels slow

Stressed

my brain feels full
and my stomach
feels tight

Stress meter

The **green to orange zone** is where they feel just right. Ask them how their brains and their bodies feel (refer to the body images in the chart on the previous page to help). Write those words on the stress meter. Take a photo of the 'calm' student if that helps.

Finally, the **stress zone** on the right needs to be completed. Have each student describe how their brain and their body feel – where in the body do they feel stress? Selfies are often helpful and can add a bit of humor to the discussion.

Add the dial/hand (included in the appendix along with a blank stress meter).

Have each student turn the dial to their current stress level. Practice mindful breathing and do a 'check-in'. Ask each student to turn the dial to represent their current level. See what's changed (or not) and discuss what they learned and what they need to do.

I love using Biodots® to add more feedback on how each student feels. Biodots®[7] are small self-adhesive circles that change color based on body temperature. You place one on the web of skin between your thumb and index finger. They can give a rough gauge of your emotional state. They're a fun way to increase self-awareness of rising stress. They can help with ongoing monitoring as the student checks in over time.

3. Improve ability to self-regulate mood

Ways to get un-bored

Once each student has completed their own stress meter, it's time to figure out ways to get themselves to an optimal 'just right' level. They need to start noticing the warning signals and do something to help themselves.

If they're feeling bored, ask them what they can do to help themselves feel less bored ('just right'). Some students need intense stimulation, like heavy physical workout, in order to alert themselves. Other students need calming and centering activities to prepare them for learning. It's really individual.

Here are some suggestions for students with different needs:

- Deep-muscle stimulation to alert themselves like doing jumping jacks, push-ups on the floor, jumping on a trampoline, wall push-ups, pressing hands into each other (isometric exercise), sitting on a therapy ball, running, skipping.
- Movement like walk around, stand up, go and get a drink.
- Nutrition like having a drink or snack.
- Brain alerting like thinking about one of their favorite people, animals, places or activities, wiping their face with cool water.

Have each student choose one or two strategies. Then prompt them to add them to their stress meters so they have a reminder.

Ways to get de-stressed

Regulating stress simply isn't going to happen all the time. We're people, not robots. But there are strategies each student can use to return to 'just right'.

Here are some strategies students can use when they find themselves in the eye of the storm. These are ways they can help themselves when they're starting to feel frustrated, frightened, or angry and need to regain a sense of calm and equilibrium.

The first step is always to stop, think, then breathe. This process helps them calm and centre themselves before selecting a specific strategy. Use visual reminders like the one shown on the next page. These can be posted on each student's desk and/or in a central location in the classroom.

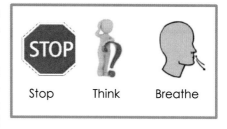

Stop   Think   Breathe

A note of caution is needed though: if emotions are already high, go directly to a strategy. I know for myself that if someone tells me to calm down when my emotions are high, it can just make it worse.

Generally, it's best to teach the strategies when the children are calm and rested. Choose a quiet time and space to introduce and to practice each one. But, be careful how you present the idea. You don't want to remind children about a worry or fear (for example, "You remember when that big dog growled at you?").

There are four main ways to help children self-regulate their mood more effectively in tough situations. They include:

1. **Distract**. This involves thinking about something pleasant. The goal with Distracting is to help children switch their focus from some worry or concern to something pleasant and calming.

   You can use modeling, like "When I'm feeling worried, I think about my favorite things." You can also prompt the child, "Let's think about something you love. How about ....?"

   I've taught children to think about their favorite Pokémon character, their pet, a favorite person or anything/anyone that makes them feel happy. I recall one boy who became agitated because

   he saw some Pokémon stickers and couldn't get them out of his mind. Pokémon was his favorite thing in the world. He got more and more agitated. He kept saying how Pokémon was all he could think about. He couldn't do anything else. I sat with him and told him how sometimes thinking about my dog made my brain feel calmer. I knew he also had a dog he adored. As soon as he thought of his dog, he forgot about Pokémon.

   Introduce the idea of thinking about a favorite thing. With the child's help, draw a thought bubble with a picture, drawing or photo of the child's favorite thing. Practice looking at and thinking about the favorite thing and making your brain and body feel calm. Combine this with mindful breathing to enhance the effect. Then when you see the child becoming upset, remind them to think of the favorite thing or just point to their thought bubble.

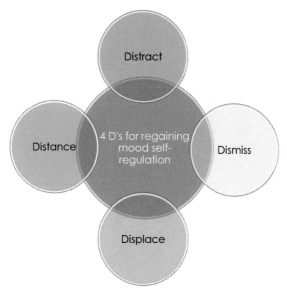

Four ways to regain mood self-regulation

2. **Dismiss**. This means getting rid of or putting away the thing that's causing distress. The idea is that you can take things out of your brain so they don't bother you anymore.

   I've used this strategy mainly when worries come up. I've also used it when thoughts seem to be buzzing around in the child's brain, making it difficult for them to think of anything else. Prompt the child: "It looks like that's really bugging your brain (referring to a thought or idea). How about we take it out. That way it won't bug you anymore." Then reach up and pretend to pull the idea out of the child's head. This should be done with great sincerity and respect.

   There are a few different things you can do with the worry you now hold in your hand. I always ask children what they want to do – do they want to put it in the garbage or flush it down the toilet? Would they prefer to shred it or destroy it in some way? Do they want to put it away for later? I always have a Brain Box© for this.

A Brain Box© is any special container where ideas can be kept. I usually buy them at the dollar store. We write or draw the

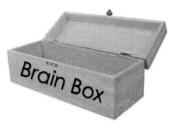

idea/worry on a piece of paper and then put it in the box. Then close in the box to seal it in.

Brain Boxes© are amazingly powerful. I told a preschool teacher about this and she thought I was mad. One day, however, a child came to preschool singing a song over and over. The teacher couldn't stop him. Then, she remembered the Brain Box©. In desperation, she said to the child, "It looks like those words are making it hard for your brain to think. How about if we take them out?" He was okay with that idea so she reached over and motioned to pull them out of his head. She then put them in her pocket (she didn't have a Brain Box© yet). The child stopped singing the song ... for the next 2 1/2 hours! When his bus came for him at the end of class, the teacher heard him screaming. She rushed to him and he said, "I need my words back!" The teacher put her hand into her pocket, pulled the imaginary words out and placed them back in his head. The child left happily singing his song once again.

There are other ways to dismiss ideas and worries. Use a shield to

keep unwanted things away. I've made shields with children to help them know they can keep some things from bugging them, just like soldiers, warrior princesses, and knights. They can hold up their shields and things just bounce right off. That way, the troublesome things can't even get near them.

You can also use other barriers, like traffic cones. I used traffic cones with a child who was afraid of monsters coming to get him during the night. I talked to him about a few strategies and he liked the idea of traffic cones best. We bought some at the dollar store. He helped set them up around his bed. He slept soundly after that.

These simple devices help dismiss concerns. They help children feel in control of things that are making it hard for them to be calm and feel 'just right'.

3. **Displace.** The child decides to put the problem or worry away until another time. The goal with Displacing is to help children put a worry or problem away for another time.

I found myself working on a project the other day. I realized that

 my frustration was increasing. Things weren't heading in a good direction. What was my solution? I decided to try again tomorrow. That's displacing the activity. I wasn't going to abandon it. I just thought a little break would help refresh my enthusiasm and patience.

We can help children do this too. When you see children becoming worried or frustrated, introduce the idea of leaving it for right now. This can be a brief or longer break. Suggest "How about we put that away for right now?" Follow this with an explanation, like "It's pretty late in the day to do something like this." or "I think your brain needs a little break." or "I think we need ____ to help do this because they're an expert." Make a plan for when and where they'll try again. Then calmly put the worry, thought or activity away and do something relaxing or refreshing.

I've also developed 'Take 5' bags with students. The bags contain a variety of things that can calm them. Contents vary by student but typical things include chewing gum, chewy object, or food, a favorite book, coloring book with markers or crayons. They're meant to be things that help them take a little quiet time to rest their worries and focus on their senses.

Some schools have specially designated sensory rooms where students can go to regain equilibrium. There can be other quiet places for students to go, such as the library or quiet corner in the Resource room.

PASS

Good for
for a 5-minute break

Start a pass system so you can keep track of students. You can make up passes like that shown to the left. If a student detects rising distress (or boredom), they can take a pass and quietly go to a quiet place. Students can come and get a pass from you to spend five minutes regaining calm alertness. Also, if you notice that a student is becoming agitated, you can quietly explain that it looks like they need a break and hand them a card.

4. **Distance**. This means mentally stepping away from the problem and looking at it like an outsider would.

The goal with Distancing is to help children learn to stand back from a situation or problem. Then they can look at it more objectively, with less emotion.

Sound odd? There's lots of science behind it. Self-distancing has been used for decades to help people get a better perspective on problems. You've heard people say to themselves, "What would Mom/Dad do in this situation?" That's distancing. It helps to step back, cool down, and evaluate things with less emotion.

Children can be taught to do the same thing. A delightful study[8] was done to look at how distancing helped preschoolers self-regulate. Some were taught to talk to themselves by name ("Okay, Heather, what are you going to do now."). Others were taught to take the perspective of a favorite media character and ask themselves, "What would Batman do?" For experimental control, another group was left to do what they usually do. The results were clear: talking to yourself was pretty good at helping self-regulation. But, thinking like a media character was most helpful. They found, though, for children to benefit the most, they needed to have stronger Theory of Mind (that is, be able to think how someone else thinks).

Lots of children with exceptional learning needs are delayed in developing Theory of Mind so what can we do? I use another form of

distancing that doesn't need much Theory of Mind. I've found that, by prompting children to talk to their brain, feet, hands, mouth, they can more calmly control them. It started one time when a child ripped up a craft. I said, "Oh, look what you did." The child looked at me ready to cry. I felt horrid. My job was to teach them, not make them cry. I quickly corrected myself and said, "Look what your hands did.

They forgot to be gentle. Let's teach those hands how to be gentle." It worked! The student looked at their hands and said, "Be gentle." They continued to work with a new sense of pride and command over their hands.

If a child puts their hand in paint, what can you do to get them to regain self-regulation? Prompt them by saying, "Oh my goodness, look what your hand did. It forgot that brushes are for paint. Tell your hand that brushes are for paint." This encourages children to distance themselves and act as the masters of their body. It helps them stay calm and to take control.

I've used distancing with swearing and mean words ("Those swears/mean words just slipped out of your mouth. How can you help your mouth?"), running ("I think your feet forgot to walk. What can you tell your feet"), gentle touching ("What do we tell your hands when you pat the kitten? That's right, be gentle, hands."), and in many other situations. By putting our children in the driver's seat with their own self-regulation, they feel a greater sense of power and are more likely to use it.

Below and on the next page are some books that can be used with young children to introduce each of the four D's. You can find more by searching a wonderful database[9] of children's books at Miami University. Search by keywords like 'bravery', 'challenges', 'determination', 'courage', 'persistence'. Books on these themes will be shown along with a short summary about each story.

Here are some examples of books that can help young children learn strategies for regaining self-regulation. There are many possibilities but I've included a few of my favorites.

Distract
The Kissing Hand by Audrey Penn - this is a delightful children's book about a raccoon who was worried about starting school. His mother gives his hand a kiss so, if he feels worried, he can look at his hand and remember his mother loves him. Age 3 to 8 years.

Dismiss
The Little Old Lady Who Was Not Afraid of Anything by Linda Williams – charming story about a woman who was confronted by scary objects but she stood up to each one. Age 4 to 8 years.

Go Away, Big Green Monster by Ed Emberley - simple little book that teaches 'power language' ("Go Away") to each scary element. Age 2 to 5 years.

Displace

***The Queen's Feet* by Sarah Ellis** - this is one of my favorite books because it deals positively with a problem behavior (the queen's busy feet). The final resolution is to let her feet be busy at certain times only. Age 4 to 6 years.

***Alexander and the Terrible, Horrible, No Good, Very Bad Day* by Judith Little** - everything seems to go wrong for Alexander but he learns that somethings like this just happen (even in Australia). Age 6 to 9 years.

Distance

***The Little Engine that Could* by Watty Piper** - this is a good book to help children think like the Little Engine - it kept going and telling itself "I think I can". Age 3 to 8 years.

***Chester the Brave* by Audrey Penn** - in this book the Little is nervous about trying things. His mother teaches him to talk to himself and say he can do it. Age 3 to 8 years.

Books for older children are a little easier to find. Ask a librarian for novels that use the 4 D's.

Mindful breathing every day

Integrate mindful breathing into everyday classroom life. You might take the first two minutes of each class to do mindful breathing with everyone. Doing it as a group will ensure that everyone benefits.

It's important to teach students to do periodic check-ins with themselves. You might just prompt everyone, "Let's check in". You can do it at specific times, like before a class starts or mid-way through a lesson. At these check-ins, show your own level on the stress meter to the students and have everyone share theirs. Use this time to remind them of strategies for staying in the optimal ('just right') zone.

---

[3] Mindfulness comes from Buddhist teachings but the way you'll present it and practice it is completely secular.

[4] Go to https://www.relaxmelodies.com/

[5] Keep in mind that apps come and go. Some stop working when operating systems change. Some are no longer available for other reasons.

[6] Source: Nummenmaa, L., Hari, R., Hietanen, J. K., & Glerean, E. (2018). Maps of subjective feelings. *Proceedings of the National Academy of Sciences*, 201807390. https://doi.org/10.1073/pnas.1807390115

[7] Purchase Biodots® through https://biodots.net/ or locate them elsewhere on the internet.

[8] White, R. E., & Carlson, S. M. (2016). What would Batman do? Self-distancing improves executive function in young children. *Developmental Science, 19*(3), 419–426. https://doi.org/10.1111/desc.12314

[9] Children's Picture Book Database at Miami University https://dlp.lib.miamioh.edu/picturebook/

Chapter

6

Dealing with specific behaviors

Sometimes you'll identify specific behaviors that are problems. Before trying to help change them, you need a clear idea of what's going on, how the student views it, and what you want to happen.

Gathering information (the detective work) is the first step in effectively dealing with specific behaviors. You have to get a clear picture of what's going on and how the student sees things.

Here are the steps:

- **Identify one issue or situation** that's a problem for the student. Work on just one behavior at a time.

- **Watch your student** and/or discreetly interview other people who know them well. Try to define:

  - where the problem tends to happen,

  - when the problem tends to happen,

  - who's involved,

  - how the issue or situation tends to begin and end,

  - what the nature of the difficulty seems to be,

  - what your student does and what the other person/people do, and

  - what might motivate your student to respond as they do. You can use the *Motivation Assessment Scale* (MAS)[10] to help. The MAS helps narrow down whether the behavior is a result of sensory issues, need to escape, a desire for attention, wanting something tangible. It doesn't include all possibilities but it may help you review and, perhaps revise, your assumptions.

- **Interview the student** and others who know them well. This'll help you understand the student's perspective and their understanding of the issue or situation. Use neutral language, being careful not to point fingers or make the student feel defensive. Introduce the idea as an observation ("Sometimes, I see that when X happens, you ..."). One student told me she didn't want to do a certain activity because it was "boring". I asked her to help me understand what that meant. It turned out that she really meant that the tasks were too difficult for her to do. She had fine motor difficulties and she had chosen to call the challenging activities "boring", perhaps to save face. Try to figure out:

  - what the student understands of the situation or issue, remembering to probe their use of words like "boring", "stupid", "babyish" because there may be more to those labels than their surface meaning,

  - what they believe motivates this behavior, and

  - what cues they notice or focus on – be aware that it can be very different from what you notice.

- **Clearly define the goal** (what you want your student to do). Figure out what background knowledge and skills your student needs to understand in order to be successful in using the strategy. Ask yourself if, given your student's background knowledge and skills, should you proceed with this behavior or should you take a step or two back to establish a firmer foundation of skills and knowledge.

- **Evaluate the strategy** in terms of:

  - **Potential consequence** for your student if they successfully use it. Think of yourself as an alien, landing on Earth who knows nothing about your culture. If the alien followed every word of the strategy, would they be successful in navigating the situation? Figure out what they need to focus on. Which things are most important and meaningful to the student?

  - **Things that might change** in the situation. Could the people change? How about the location or time? Figure out how to build these changes into your strategy so the student can still follow it.

- **How appropriate it is to the student's age, peer group, and culture.** An important part of helping students develop skills is to ensure that they're age-, peer-, and/or culturally appropriate. Watch their peers and see how they behave and what they say in similar situations. Strategies are meant to help students, not make them stand out or appear awkward. I remember therapists teaching children to say, "Can I play with you?" in order to join others. It looked a little odd so I watched what other children their age did. I found that only as a last resort did children actually ask others to play. They generally just stood close by and looked interested. Very often other children noticed and let them join in. If looking interested didn't work, the next step was to comment on the play. These were often comments about how nice a toy was. Rarely, did a child ask to play. I used this information to form more appropriate strategies for students.

- **How to incorporate your student's interests.** By including areas of high interest, you're more likely to gain their attention. I mocked up a driver's licence for one student who loved cars. The licence looked fairly authentic but, on the back, were the steps they needed to follow. They were thrilled to carry it (of course, I made clear that this didn't mean they could actually drive).

Now that you have a clearer understanding of the behavior, select a strategy to address it.

There are four main types of strategies you can use to help resolve specific problem behaviors. They include:

1. Simple behavior rules

2. Expanded behavior rules

3. Social Stories™

4. Problem solving

Each of these can be used individually or in combination. Try the different approaches and decide which are more effective in dealing with certain types of behaviors or with specific students.

1. Simple behavior rules

Simple behavior rules detail the behavior you want and, sometimes, where to use it.

Find a positive name for the behavior you've chosen. I've found that if you call it "not swearing", say, some students will simply focus on 'swearing'. If you name it "use kind words", they'll focus on "kind words" – that's our goal.

Explain to the student in positive terms what you've noticed and how it impacts him and other people. It's important the student understand the meaning and purpose to any changes. For example, you can explain that you've noticed they stand really close to other people when they talk. That makes other people uncomfortable and they don't want to talk with them. People prefer if you stand about one arm's-length away. Ask the student how to write a rule for that so they can remember.

Stand one arm away

If it's in their own words, they're more likely to have a sense of ownership. Always write out the rule and pair it with some visual reminder (like the example to the left). You might include a picture of their favorite media character, their best friend or them demonstrating the rule (rather than clipart like I used).

Practice the rule by acting out scenarios with the student. Take turns so the student has a chance to remind you. It just feels so much better when you're not the only one who forgets sometimes! Make sure you practice enough so both you and the student get a chance to remind each other of the rule. Tell them they can remind themselves and you but no one else. We don't want them to become a 'policeman' for everyone else's behavior.

Introduce the rule into daily life. Be sure to let the student know when they're following the rule. Just go up to them and say you noticed how well they're remembering. There'll also be times when you need to remind them to use the rule – they'll slip up like anyone else. Make sure you remind them in private and respectful ways. Also try to praise them more than remind them. That is, let them know they're following the rule more often than not. If the student ignores the rule or purposely violates it, sit down with them, discuss the issues and try to reach a renewed understanding or a compromise. Remind them of the social consequence of forgetting to use the rule, such as 'other people won't want to be around you.'

Here are two examples:

When talking about very personal issues, there are appropriate times and places. This isn't obvious to many students with autism. Define places where they shouldn't share their personal stories. These are places where they're free from personal information – they're 'free zones' – notice that the wording is positive. Discuss the need for the rule and write it with the student. You can post a visual like the one to the right to help guide the student's behavior and remind them. This means also that there are zones where they can discuss personal issues. Always have a balance between places where students can do something and where they need to self-regulate.	**Personal information Free Zone** 
"*stim zone*" – students on the autism spectrum usually have some 'stimming' behaviors. Their stims can be viewed as weird and marginalizing by other students so you want to help the student find appropriate times and places to stim. The idea is that stims are pleasurable releases so we help students find time for them. Find a location where the student can go and stim. That's the Stim Zone. Discuss the need for the rule and write it with the student. Then you can post a visual like the one to the right to help guide the student's behavior and remind them. You'll notice a piece of string in the picture to the right. Twirling a piece of string is a common stim.	Stim zone

2. Expanded Behavior Rules

This approach expands rules to include definition of the issue and steps needed to address it. The Expanded Behavior Rule format is more specific about when, where, and with whom the problem arises. It also defines the reason for the rule. Perhaps most importantly, it presents ways the student can help themselves remember to use the rule.

Write the Expanded Behavior Rule in the first person as if the student was writing it themselves. The information should always reflect the student's perspective of the situation.

Use positive language. Avoid negatives as much as possible. Never mention the undesirable behavior unless absolutely unavoidable. That is, don't say "stop swearing" or "don't run away". Mentioning the undesirable behavior can simply reinforce it. Use neutral words to describe any undesired behavior to avoid arousing your student's anxiety.

Here's an example (a blank form is in Appendix II):

3. Social Stories™

Social Stories™ are explanations of social rules and routines in a story format. They are similar to Expanded Behavior Rules but present the information in a story.

The creator of Social Stories™, Carol Gray, specifies steps you need to

---

Behavior rule: _what to do when someone is bugging me_

Definition: _bugging means that something the person is doing or saying is making it hard for me to think & feel okay_

When: _when I feel distracted and it's hard to think and to feel comfortable_

Where: _in class, during breaks_

Who's there: _Jon, Celine, Chris_

What to say and do:
1. _stop, stay calm, and think about what I can do to help myself_
2. _ignore the other person_
3. _if it doesn't stop, say, "I don't like it when you do that."_
4. _if the person still doesn't stop, I leave and go to another place_
5. _if the person is still bugging me, I tell a teacher or supervisor_

Reasoning: _I do this because I can think better when I'm calm and I can help other people understand when something is bugging me_

How I can help myself remember: _I can make a picture of a shield in my head – that'll help me ignore the other person_

---

follow in order to write an effective Social Story™. Take the time to complete each step. That way, you'll end up with better quality and more effective stories.

Carol also prefers for you to write the first story about a skill or situation that is typically successful and problem-free for the student. Then the student will associate positive experiences with these stories. That is, not all Social Stories™ are for telling them how to do something differently. She suggests that at least half of all future stories should draw attention to positive things the student has done. Use your judgement about this.

Write the story in the first person as if the student was writing it themselves.

Use positive language. Avoid negatives as much as possible. Never include undesirable behavior unless absolutely unavoidable (don't include things like "sometimes I hit other people"). Use neutral words to describe any undesired behavior to avoid increasing your student's anxiety. I remember a boy whose teacher wrote a Social Story™ addressing his tendency to run off on his own. She titled the story, "I should not run away." The boy showed me the book and excitedly said, "Look, there's me running away!" He thought it was funny and the title just reinforced his behavior. Needless to say, I changed the title to "How I stay with adults."

Title. Write a title that's positive and describes the overall idea being addressed. When you write a title, make sure it describes what you want and not want you don't want. Notice in the example on page 43, the focus is on being a leader rather than on being the centre of attention,

Introduction. Start with a sentence that introduces the topic in terms of the general rule (e.g. Sometimes, people need to ...) or a motivation statement (e.g. I like ...).

The example story on page 43 states:

> *"I have many good ideas. I have lots of things I know in my brain."*

Next statement. Define any terms used if needed (e.g. X means ...).

The example story uses this statement:

> *"Sometimes, adults ask me to be a leader. They want me to help other kids do or say things".*

Main body. Describe what people typically do in the situation, the setting, or activity. Also add people who are involved. State why people do these things. Make sure the statements are truthful and don't assume anything. Spell out the details if they need explanation.

Be sure to include conditional words (e.g. "usually", "sometimes", "might") so the student knows that nothing happens all the time or with total certainty.

Examples from the story on page 43 are:

"They might ask me to stand up. Then I have to do or say something. The other kids will stay sitting down."

"They might ask me to be in the centre of a circle. They might ask me to be the only person who does something."

These statements are setting the stage for expectations.

Include a statement that gives a reason for the behavior. Here's what I stated in the story on page 43:

"My friends can watch me and learn some of the things in my brain."

I chose to put the reason for the behavior a little later in the story because it seemed to flow better.

Closing. Provide a **directive** statement. These explain what an appropriate response or choice of responses is.

Examples from the story on page 43:

"Sometimes I feel nervous and I say "no thanks". Next time a teacher asks me to be a leader, I will stay calm. I will tell my brain that being a leader helps my friends learn."

Conclusion. End with an **affirmative** statement that gives more meaning by stating shared values and opinions (e.g. ____ is a very important thing to do). Here's what I wrote in the example story:

"The other kids will like to hear my ideas. They can learn the things I know. My teacher will be happy because I helped her teach the other kids."

and/or **control** statement that identifies personal strategies to help the student remember the story and strategies (e.g. I will tell my brain to remember ...).

The example social story below was written for a student who didn't like to be singled out. I used the term 'leader' because it's positive and places the student in a leadership role. The student liked to tell others what to do so I focused on that, rather than the idea of being singled out.

There are examples of Social Stories™ on the internet but many aren't very well written. Some on Carol Gray's website[11] are quite effective but be selective. Some are better quality than others.

How to be a Good Leader By John Smith	I have many good ideas. I have lots of things I know in my brain.
Sometimes, adults ask me to be a leader. They want me to help other kids do or say things.	They might ask me to stand up. Then I have to do or say something. The other kids will stay sitting down.
They might ask me to be in the centre of a circle. They might ask me to be the only person who does something.	Sometimes I feel nervous and I say "no thanks".
Next time a teacher asks me to be a leader, I will stay calm. I will tell my brain that being a leader helps my friends learn.	My friends can watch me and learn some of the things in my brain.
The other kids will like to hear my ideas. They can learn the things I know.	My teacher will be happy because I helped her teach the other kids.

4. Teach problem solving

This is a process that teaches students to analyze and act on problems they come across. If they learn how to reflect on and solve problems on their own, they've made solid steps toward becoming independent adults.

The problem-solving process is always taught when students are calm – not in the middle of a problem. To teach the process, start with something fairly neutral and straightforward. You might choose something from your own life (for example, I keep losing my car keys) so it doesn't

43

inject any stress or anxiety into your teaching. Then take the student through the process of helping you solve your problem

The process is as follows:

1. **What's the problem?** Define the problem carefully with the student, using clear, simple, positive language. Take time to do this. It's critical that the issues are clearly spelled out so that everyone understands them. Students with autism often focus on things that are the most important features. It's important that you help them with this.

2. **What could I do?**

   Plan: Together with the student, brainstorm up to three possible things they could do to solve the problem. In the learning stages, accept any suggestions – even ones that might seem a little odd. Part of the learning process is to weed out good from not-great ideas.

   What might happen? Figure out, with the student, what might happen if they used each one of the plans. Look at both logical and emotional consequences, including how they might feel and how other people might feel. Act each one out if that might help.

3. **Which one will I try?** Help the student decide which one of the three suggested solutions they might try out. In the early stages, you might try all three ideas (one at a time) just to experience the outcomes. Help evaluate the potential impact of each choice on relationships with other people. Let them try any of the possible solutions – more learning can sometimes occur when trying out 'not great' ideas.

4. **What will I say and do?**

   Say: Be careful not to assume that, once they've decided on a plan, the student knows what to do. Help them script out what they'll say when using their plan.

   Do: Write out each step and act it out with the student so they can judge the potential effectiveness.

5. **How did it work?** After the student has tried their plan, help them evaluate how it worked. Include both logical consequences (such as, did they get what they wanted), and emotional consequences (such as, what was the impact on other people).

6. **Should I try something else?** Ask the student is they might try some-thing else or are they satisfied with the current plan. First, re-exam-ine the definition of the problem to make sure it's accurate. Then look at other possible solutions and try again.

Give the student as much leeway in this problem-solving process as you feel appropriate. Sometimes, letting the student experience a mildly negative response can lead to effective learning. For example, if the student decides that covering their mouth when they burp is a better plan than suppressing it or going elsewhere, let them try it out to see what happens.

Expect the students to start using the Problem-Solving format on their own only after repeated practice. They'll initially need a lot of support. Typically, the greatest challenges for students with autism are defining the problem and figuring out how plans might impact other people.

An example Problem-Solving process is shown on the next page (a blank form is included in Appendix II).

No matter what approach you use

Always keep in mind, first steps should always:

- Define desired behavior <u>with</u> each student. This will help you un-derstand the student's perspective. You'll learn what you need to help them focus on.

  State the desired behavior in positive terms. Never describe it in terms of what the student does. Instead of saying "running away', "screaming in the bathroom", or "hitting other people", say "staying with my teacher", "using a quiet voice", and "us-ing gentle hands."

- Use vocabulary and concepts the student understands. I find that using a readability analysis[12] is helpful. The analysis shows you the reading level of what you've written. That's defined in terms of average sentence length and the number of more complicated words.

- Avoid punishing problem behavior (for example, by taking away privileges) unless absolutely necessary. That means, you've done everything possible to teach the student and to help prevent it. Once you've used up all options, you may have to resort to a negative consequence.

What's the problem?	Sometimes I want to tell other people how to do things, even when it's not my job. That's really annoying to other people and they don't want to be around me.	
What could I do?	**Plan**	**What might happen?**
	1. Say nothing	1. Things might not get done the right way.
	2. Tell my teacher	2. My teacher might not tell the other person.
	3. Write a note to the other person	3. The person might not like being told what to do.
Which one will I try?	Say nothing	
What will I say and do?	**Say:** Nothing	**Do:** 1. Remind myself: "It's not my job." 2. Remind myself: "It's okay if they do it in a different way than me."
How did it work? OK? **Should I try something else?**	It was difficult to keep my ideas in my head but I did it. My teacher said I did a good job. No one got angry with me. This is hard to do but other people were happier. I guess this is the best thing to do right now.	

- Practice and review each rule, story, or problem-solving process many times. Students need to review them, often on at least a daily basis, before they should be expected to use them on their own.

- Use visual reminders to help recall strategies and procedures on their own. These can be simple cue cards, fake drivers' licences, or whatever you can dream up with the student.

- Work on one behavior at a time. Help your student master one behavior before moving on to something else. I met a child whose well-meaning teachers had written 52 Social Stories™ for her. This small library was reviewed on a rotating basis. Fifty-two is way too many for anyone to recall.

To help you work with each student, a **Quick Checklist** of steps to take is included in Appendix III.

Promoting generalization of rules and strategies

The ultimate goal is to have the student use rules and strategies independently in everyday situations. We also want them to learn to deal with other problems in life. The most effective way to do this is to encourage students to think on their own. Prompt them to recall rules and strategies. Ask them to think of ways to help themselves. Don't feel you have to come up with all the ideas.

Below and on the next page are some examples of teacher responses that either stop or promote thinking. When teachers tell students what to do, the students become passive. That means they're not thinking on their own and they aren't being prepared for adult life. But, when teachers ask the student to think for themselves, they're helping them become more effective problem-solvers.

Situation	Student is Passive recipient	Active problem-solving by the student
You're working with a group of students and other students are being too noisy	"Be quiet. You're making too much noise"	"We're having a hard time hearing. What could you do to help us?"
It's the end of a class or the day	"Put your things away and don't forget your home-work...."	"What do you need to do to get yourself ready to leave?"
One student is distracting another	"Move away from Kim."	"Kim, it looks like you're having a hard time listening. What could you do to help yourself?"
A student is making loud noises while another is trying to talk	"Be quiet"	"I think it is Mary's turn to talk. What could we do to help her?"
A student volunteers to help you	"Get ten pieces of paper. Pass one piece to each student ...."	"Let's look at what we've planned. What kind of things do you think we need? Can you make sure everyone gets what they need?"
A student interrupts while you're talking to someone else	"Don't interrupt"	"I'm talking to Barb and I want to hear her. What could you do if you need to talk?"
A student pushes ahead of another student in a line.	"Don't push"	"How are we supposed to line up?", "How do we treat our friends?"

Notice how teachers who promote active problem-solving use open-ended questions. These are questions that don't have a simple 'yes' or 'no' answer. They require some thinking.

---

[10] You can find the *Motivation Assessment Scale* online at https://coe.uoregon.edu/cds/files/2018/01/Motivational-Assessment-Scale-II.pdf

[11] https://carolgraysocialstories.com/social-stories/

[12] I find this automatic readability checker very useful: http://www.readabilityformulas.com/free-readability-formula-tests.php

Regaining Equilibrium

It's difficult to prevent all incidents. A student may quickly slip into a state of distress and be unable to activate their strategies. So, what do you do?

It's most important to focus on helping the student regain calmness and preserving their reputation and dignity as much as possible.

Calming strategies

Quiet, calm assistance, reassurance, and quiet time can help sometimes.

I've found a few things that can help students regain a sense of calm. Here are some examples that typically work:

Typical Calming Strategies for students with autism	Examples
Quiet help with some of the details and facts that are overwhelming them; organizing and accomplishing small projects or steps	"How about if we do this part tomorrow?"; "How about if you do that part and I'll do the other part?"; covering up or removing parts of a task
Time to recognize connections between a new event or activity and other experiences	"This is just like that work you did the other day.", "This is about .... You know a lot about that.",
Getting away from the stress	Time in a quiet space
Time alone in a pleasant sensing environment	Time in a sensory room; time with companion animal; using their Take 5 bag; listening to calming music
Specific and concrete validation of their competence and worth	"You have a really good brain. Let's just take a breath and try again."
Reminding them of previous positive outcomes	"Remember the last time this happened, you fixed things up really well and did great work."

Headlong into distress

There will be times when a student goes quickly into distress. It's unlikely you can stop it. Things may actually escalate if you try to intervene. The student just has to play out the stress reaction before being able to re-group and try again.

The acronym R.E.S.T.O.R.E.[13] can help you remember what to do to help students get back to a state of equilibrium. R.E.S.T.O.R.E. includes most of the calming strategies in the table on the previous page but gives you a sequence to follow.

Relax, get rid of any thoughts about the possible reason(s) why the student behaved the way they did – **reframe** the student's behavior in neutral terms about what happened, NOT why!

Empathize with them and **express** your concern for the student and their feelings – "I'm sorry you're upset. Sometimes things just get difficult." Don't talk too much. Keep your discussion short and simple.

Soothe them **silently**, say little or nothing; **sense** their heart rate and breathing to track the student's stress reaction.

Time alone helps the student calm down; allow them to do nothing or do something that's less stimulating. You can give them the option of leaving the space but it may be too much for them to handle at that moment.

Organize the task or activity into smaller, more 'do-able' pieces while the student is calming down; it's usually wise to organize the task/activity out of the student's line of vision so sight of it doesn't set them off again.

Reinforce their feelings of competence, tell them in as few words as possible how they've been successful before; prompt them to tell themselves how well they can do and how it takes time to learn.

Entice them to the task or activity, such as by asking them for help, talking about interesting things about the activity; if they're calm, encourage them to think about what they could do next time to help themselves.

Here is one example of how to apply the R.E.S.T.O.R.E. process:

	A task is placed in front of John and immediately he melts down and says, "No, no, I don't want to do that! I don't like it."
R	**Relax.** Your immediate response is "Well, fella, you can do it and you're just trying to avoid work today!" Stop yourself. Get rid of every judgement about John's behavior and reasons why he might be behaving this way. Look at John objectively as a person in distress who's trying to communicate something. Facial expressions of students with autism are usually not a good way to judge their feelings. DO NOT start thinking about what you may or may not have done correctly or what errors you made – this isn't the time. Take a deep breath, count to five and calm yourself. Remember that students with autism tend to be 'emotional sponges'. If you become agitated, your stress is likely just to add to John's state. If John is thrashing around or hitting out, quietly and calmly remove any objects or people from the immediate area.
E	**Empathize.** Say things like, "I'm sorry you're upset.", "I want to help you."
S	**Soothe.** Sit back and let John calm down a little. If the student responds to back rubs, try that.
T	**Time.** Give him some quiet time. You might offer him some water or juice or a piece of food. If John's presence is interfering with other students' work, offer to take him to a quiet space. Don't push, just offer – he may not be ready yet and distress could escalate again.
O	**Organize.** Now is the time to look at the task you wanted him to do and decide what would constitute 'done'. You can change the number of things he needs to do ("Let's do one more"), the difficulty of the task ("How about we try this one."), the amount of time he needs to spend on the task ("Let's do this for one more minute and then you'll be done). Change whatever is needed to give him (and you) a sense of accomplishing something.
R	**Reinforce.** Tell John, "You've got a really good brain and I know you can do this work really well. Sometimes it's a little bit hard but you can just tell yourself to stay calm and try again."
E	**Entice.** Now you can entice John back to the task. You may also decide that the work is just too much for John at that moment, especially if it is a new concept or something more difficult. At that point, say something like, "Oh my, I guess I got confused. This work is for another day. Here is the one we were supposed to do."

> You might try enticing him back by pointing to something he knows or likes: "Hey, look at this, this is the same one you did the other day. It'll be a snap."
>
> You may also entice him by commenting on what's next after he finishes this task. Build it up by saying something like, "Wow, after this you get to go to gym/music/...."

The 'Crisis Plan'

Sometimes, you simply don't have the time or you're not in a good location to try these techniques. You may be in a time crunch and not have the resources available to restore the student's equilibrium. You may be in a busy place and don't want to embarrass your student or receive advice and judgement from people around you. The student's behavior may also be causing distress for other people.

You should always have a 'crisis plan'. If the student is melting down in the middle of a public place, try clearing the area as much as possible. Remove anything that might hurt them. Tell onlookers to move on. Try your best to ignore well-meaning 'critics' and 'advisors'. Some people seem to need to give advice or criticize the student and you. Just tell them the student has special needs and you know what you're doing.

Don't talk too much or try to reason with the student. Once they're distressed, their ability to process information is compromised. Talking too much can make things worse.

The Aftermath

Once the melt down is over, it's over. I've found that most of the time, students with autism don't remember what happened. It was like a huge storm blew in and now it's done.

Temple Grandin, an adult with autism, said that her temper tantrums weren't expressions of emotions. More often than not, they happened when her 'circuits' overloaded – when she'd had enough. Once her outburst was over, all of the emotions faded away.

I've found that, once the outburst is over, to the student, it's like nothing ever happened. If you try talking about it, the student may look at you and have no recollection.

Keep that in mind when you de-brief your students. They might not remember much about the outburst. They also may have no insight into why it happened. If that's the case, move on. Don't dwell on what just happened. You can work on that another time. Then you can work it into one of the four strategies presented in Chapter 6.

---

[13] Thank you to Marlene Holmgren-Lima for helping me come up with the R.E.S.T.O.R.E. process and acronym

Chapter

8

Final words

The main points I wanted to emphasize in this guide are:

- Not all behaviors are problems – be careful when deciding what needs attention.

- Students with autism have difficulties with executive functions which means they have challenges in:

  - planning and organizing themselves,

  - controlling their behavior, thinking, and emotions,

  - in remembering information,

  - self-monitoring, and

  - in thinking and behaving flexibly.

- Stress and anxiety make it more difficult for students with autism to consciously control their executive functions. Their ability to self-regulate their behavior, thinking, and emotions is really compromised when stress enters the equation.

- Students with autism need help in learning how to calm and centre themselves, to identify how they're feeling, and to regulate their moods.

- Once specific behaviors are identified as problems, they need to be examined carefully. Special attention needs to be given to how the student views the behavior. Often students with autism will have a very different 'take' on their behavior and events in their lives. That perspective is critical to consider.

- Helping students change a problem behavior must be done in positive, non-judgemental, and objective ways – no punishment, no guilt-trip, just guidance from a trusted source.

- Change takes time and practice. Develop strategies with each student and then practice them. Remind the student frequently and post visual reminders in discreet places. Don't expect students to learn and use new strategies right away. They need your support and praise when they remember to use a strategy.

- Meltdowns will happen. Make sure the student stays safe. Provide quiet, calm support but don't expect them to remember what happened or why – just move on.

Photo credits

APPENDIX I – Survey of Stressors

Survey of Stressors

Name:	Age:
Rater:	Today's Date:

Please rate how often each item acts as a stressor for your child/student by checking (✓) the appropriate column. The ratings will hep profile the most common stressors. Put an asterisk (*) beside the items that seem to cause the most intense reactions. These can be the priorities.

How often does this child/student experience stress/distress in response to each of the following:	Never	Rarely	Sometimes	Very often	Always
1. Having personal objects or materials missing					
2. Being asked to work below their own standards					
3. Being interrupted					
4. Being told "no"					
5. Having to do a new task/activity					
6. Receiving criticism or a reprimand					
7. Having to engage in back and forth conversation					
8. Being pressured to work or finish a task quickly					
9. Having a change in their schedule or plans					
10. Being around an odor that's unpleasant to them					
11. Having to do an activity/task they don't like					
12. Being prevented from focusing on an area/topic of high interest					
13. Working for long periods of time without breaks					
14. Being asked to do something without clear directions or guidance					
15. Being asked to stop repetitive (self-stim) behavior (hand-flapping, rocking, spinning)					

	Never	Rarely	Sometimes	Very often	Always
16. Feeling hungry (hasn't eating in over 2-3 hours)					
17. Having personal objects or materials disorganized or out of the normal order					
18. Being expected to work in a group with other children/students					
19. Being treated in a way that seems unfair to them					
20. Being prevented from carrying out a ritual					
21. Being given vague or unclear expectations or goals					
22. Being expected to compete with others					
23. Being praised					
24. Waiting for a reward or present					
25. Working in a way that seems sloppy to them					
26. Being exposed to a fire alarm or other sudden loud noises					
27. Spending too little time alone					
28. Being asked to do something in a different way from usual					
29. Not feeling well					
30. Having their work marked incorrect					
31. Having unstructured time					
32. Being in a place with bright lights, especially fluorescent lights					
33. Receiving hugs, affection					
34. Working with a group of other children/students					
35. Waiting for activities/events					
36. Receiving a surprise (present, unexpected visitor)					

	Never	Rarely	Sometimes	Very often	Always
37. Changing to an unfamiliar environment/setting					
38. Failure of other people to do what they said they'd do					
39. Being near noise or disruptions					
40. Attending a group event like a party					
41. Having a change in staff, teacher, assistant, etc.					
42. Being pressured to meet a deadline					
43. Being asked to do an activity/task differently once they've already started					
44. Moving from one location to another					
45. Being touched					
46. Being given too much information or having too much information around them					
47. Being separated from their family or close friend					
48. Losing at a game					
49. Being in a disorganized environment/setting					
50. Being isolated socially or not accepted by other children/students					
51. Having someone disagree about something they feel certain of					
Fears					
1. Of the dark					
2. Of water (pool, lake, ocean)					
3. Of animals					
4. Of crowds					
5. Of being left alone					
6. Of closed spaces					

	Never	Rarely	Sometimes	Very often	Always
Life Stressors					
1. Death of a close relative or friend					
2. Moving to a new school					
3. Moving to a new home					
4. Getting a haircut					
5. New person living in their home					
6. Going to the doctor or dentist					
7. Parents getting separated or divorced					
Other Stressors					
1.					
2.					
3.					
4.					
5.					
Summary of major stressors					

APPENDIX II - Stress Meter & Blank Forms

Stress Meter and dial

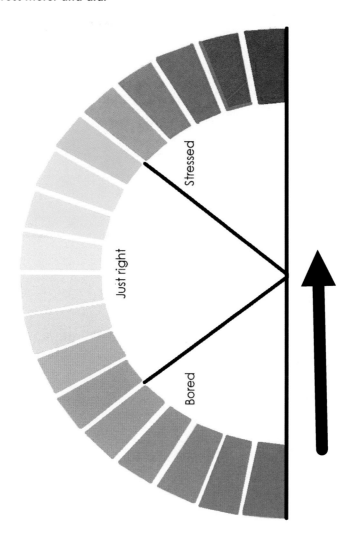

Stressed

Just right

Bored

Expanded Behavior Rule format:

Issue: _____

Definition: _____

_____

When: _____

_____

Where: _____

Who's there: _____

What to say and do:

1. _____

2. _____

3. _____

4. _____

5. _____

Reasoning: _____

_____

How I can help myself remember:_____

_____

Problem-solving format

What's the problem?			
What could I do?	**Plan** 1. 2. 3.		**What might happen?** 1. 2. 3.
Which one will I try?			
What will I say and do?	Say:		Do:
How did it work? OK **Should I try some-thing else?**			

APPENDIX III - Quick checklist to help students with their behavior

Quick Checklist		
Steps I've taken to help my student:	Yes	No
1. I've worked with the student on:		
a. Self-calming,		
b. Identifying their mood, and		
c. Self-regulating their mood.		
2. I've identified a behavior I want my student to change.		
3. I've determined that the behavior is a problem.		
4. I've watched the student and figured out:		
a. Where the behavior happens,		
b. When it happens,		
c. Who's involved,		
d. How it begins and ends,		
e. What the nature of the difficulty is,		
f. What the student does,		
g. What other people do, and		
h. What motivates the student.		
5. I've interviewed the student and others to find:		
a. What the student understands,		
b. What motivates the student, and		
c. What cues/features they focus on.		
6. I've defined with the student what they need to do differently.		
7. I've figured out if the student has the necessary background knowledge and skills.		
8. I've evaluated the strategy in relation to:		
a. What might happen if the student behaves in the new way (could it backfire?).		
b. What things might change in the situation. and		
c. The appropriateness of the behavior to the student's age, peer group, and culture.		
9. I've incorporated the student's interest area(s) into the strategy.		
a. I've chosen a strategy that		
b. Is appropriate to the behavior and to the student,		
c. Is written in positive language,		

Steps I've taken to help my student:	Yes	No
d. Incorporates visual reminders,		
e. Defines desired behavior with student input, and		
f. Uses language that is within the student's language comprehension and/or reading level.		
10. I've practiced the strategy with the student until:		
a. They show they understand it, and		
b. They can use it independently most of the time.		

About the author

Dr. Heather MacKenzie is a speech-language pathologist and educator who entered these professions 45 years ago.

She has worked as a speech-language therapist and diagnostician at the Alberta Children's Hospital (ACH) Diagnostic Assessment and Treatment Centre in Calgary, Alberta, Canada. She then went on to work for Alberta Community Health.

After obtaining her doctorate in child language, phonology, and administration of medical-educational institutions at the University of Wisconsin-Madison in the United States, Heather returned to ACH to become the Director of Preschool Services. Preschool Services provided intensive multi-disciplinary intervention for children with neurodevelopmental disorders.

In 1986, Heather opened her private speech-language practice, one of the first in Alberta. After being in private practice for over a decade, she established a preschool program for children with autism spectrum disorder, based on her Learning Preferences and Strengths model.

Heather has written five books and developed a game for enhancing conversational skills in people with autism. She has conducted workshops and given presentations throughout the U.S. and Canada, as well as the U.K., Middle East, and Asia.

Heather presently lives in the French countryside with her husband and a menagerie of dogs and cats.

Made in the
USA
Monee, IL